HALFLIFE

HALFLIFE

Meghan O'Rourke

W. W. NORTON & COMPANY
NEW YORK · LONDON

For information about permission to reproduce selections from
this book, write to Permissions, W. W. Norton & Company, Inc.
500 Fifth Avenue, New York, NY 10110

Manufacturing by Courier Westford
Book design by Chris Welch
Production manager: Julia Druskin

Library of Congress Cataloging-in-Publication Data
O'Rourke, Meghan.
Halflife : Meghan O'Rourke. —1st ed.
p. cm.
Poems.
ISBN: 978-0-393-06475-9
I. Title.
PS3615 .R586H35 2007
811' .6—dc22
2007001529

ISBN 978-0-393-33317-6 pbk.

W. W. Norton & Company, Inc.
500 Fifth Avenue
New York, N.Y. 10110
www.wwnorton.com

W. W. Norton & Company Ltd.
Castle House, 75/76 Wells Street
London W1T 3QT

1 2 3 4 5 6 7 8 9 0

FOR MY PARENTS,
BARBARA AND PAUL

The trails of light which the moths seemed to leave behind them . . . were merely phantom traces created by the sluggish reaction of the human eye . . . It was such unreal phenomena . . . the sudden incursion of unreality into the real world, certain effects of light in the landscape spread out before us, or in the eye of a beloved person, that kindled our deepest feelings, or at least what we took for them.

— *W. G. Sebald*, Austerlitz

CONTENTS

I

Meditations on a Moth   17

Sleep   18

My Life as a Teenager   19

Descent   20

Peep Show   22

Halflife   23

At Tiger Mountain   25

A Further Sea   27

War Lullaby   28

Sandy Hook   29

Elegy   30

II

Still Life Amongst Partial Outlines   33

III

Checklist   49

Epitaph for Mother and Child   50

Prayer   52

The Lighthouse Keeper   53

Late Mastery   54

Winter Palace   55

The Climber in the Ice   56

Sophomores   57

Anatomy of Failure   58

Troy   59

IV

Two Sisters   63

Westport Cemetery   71

V

Hunt   75

Stillborn   76

Thermopylae   77

Signal Fires   78

Pilgrim's Progress   79

Palimpsest   81

Spectacular   82

Inventing a Horse   83

Knives of Light   85

Notes   87

ACKNOWLEDGMENTS

Grateful acknowledgment to the editors of the following publications, in which these poems, sometimes in different forms, originally appeared:

Gulf Coast: "Late Mastery," "Palimpsest" (as "Pentimento")
The Kenyon Review: "Peep Show," "War Lullaby," "Sandy Hook,"
    part VIII of "Two Sisters," "Winter Palace"
The New Republic: "Checklist" and "Anatomy of Failure"
The New Yorker: "My Life as a Teenager," "Troy," part I of "Two
    Sisters," and "Hunt"
The New York Review of Books: "Spectacular" and "A Further Sea"
Poetry: "Halflife" and "Sleep"
Poetry Northwest: "Elegy," "Stillborn"
Slate: "Meditations on a Moth," "Descent," and part II of "Two
    Sisters"
The Yale Review: "Thermopylae"

I am indebted to the teachers and friends who generously read this manuscript in earlier drafts, and whose suggestions made it better. And to my parents—my first, beloved teachers—and my brothers. And, finally, to James Surowiecki, whose open-eyed curiosity is a continual marvel and example to me.

HALFLIFE

I

MEDITATIONS ON A MOTH

How splendid yellow is. —Vincent van Gogh

My poor eye. It has done
so much looking—at the sky, at the dark-fretted
trumpets in the frescoes of the Chrysler Building,
at the opium dens of *High and Low*,
where bodies sway like white flowers—
amount due, amount due.
Is the blue the blue you think of when I tell you?
Do ghosts have neuroses?
What is the point of the haunting they do?
Here—look. No, look.
I am trying to rid myself of myself;
to see past the tumbling clouds.
All evening drums rumble in the corner park.
The mobsters convene when the cops leave.
What goes down stays down,
the street at three A.M. a fantastic absence of color.
Outside the studio window
a river slides along its dulcimer bed,
aquifers and accordions and Alcatraz.
But you have to get up in the morning.
The brute blind glare of snow in sun.
Look again, and up you may rise
to something quite surprising in the distance.

SLEEP

Pawnbroker, scavenger, cheapskate,
come creeping from your pigeon-filled backrooms,
past guns and clocks and locks and cages,
past pockets emptied and coins picked from the floor;
come sweeping with the rainclouds down the river
through the brokenblack windows of factories
to avenues where movies whisk through basement projectors
and children peel up into the supplejack twilight
like licorice from sticky floors—
there a black-eyed straight-backed drag queen
preens, fusses, fixes her hair in a shop window on Prince,
a young businessman jingles his change
and does his Travis Bickle for a long-faced friend,
there on the corner I laughed at a joke Jim made.
In the bedroom the moon is a dented spoon,
cold, getting colder, so hurry sleep,
come creep into bed, let's get it over with;
lay me down and close my eyes
and tell me whip, tell me winnow,
tell me sweet tell me skittish
tell me No tell me no such thing
tell me straw into gold tell me crept into fire
tell me lost all my money tell me *hoarded, verboten*,
but promise tomorrow I will be profligate,
stepping into the sun like a trophy.

MY LIFE AS A TEENAGER

I felt "remorse for civilization."
My nostalgia was buoyant,
fat as cartoon clouds.
I sang teenage French, sashaying down the street:
"*Bonjour, Je t'aime, comment tu t'appelles?*"
The apartment buildings leaned down at me.
I proclaimed my love for the past,
wore fitted clothes from the 40s.
I came out against pointlessness.
All night boys danced in the living room
mouthing the words to the Go-Gos,
shrugging into the night's advances,
then took their stolen kisses from girls
fat like Troy, ready for the sieging.
In the morning, the sun was a cutout in the smog.
Every window was a picture window;
the dawn grew into day, red, orange, blue,
in perfect disorder. The partygoers were outside,
building a monument out of a blowtorch
and something old and green.
From where I stood, the tree, de-leafed and nude,
appeared to bow to me,
and what had long been silent grew.

DESCENT

I was born a bastard in an amphetamine spree,
      lit through with a mother's quickenings,

burrowing into her, afraid she would not have me,
      and she would not have me.

I dropped out down below the knees
      of a rickrack halterdress,

sheeted, tented knees, water breaking, linoleum peeling,
      and no one there to see but me,

I woke on the floor as if meant to
      put her back together, to try to hold on to her

like a crate to a river, as if I'd been shipped down
      to stand straight while in the misgiving

she said *I had a dream of thirty-six sticks*
      floating down a river and a dog who couldn't swim

and I could not swim, I slipped from her grip
      in a room where two orange cats stared

like tidy strangers at a world of larger strangeness,
      and I had no name, I was there at her breast

and I thought I could see her, the swag of her hair, the jaw,
  the fearing, but I barely saw, I went sliding down the river

from a house in which it was sweet to sleep,
  and the cool of the sheets

was never cool enough, and the imprint of the bedded bodies
  diving, at once, took the shape of two geese.

PEEP SHOW

Tokens in the slot:
ka-shot, shot, shot.
A figure in the darkness.
The tin crank
of canned do-wop.

Someone is always watching—
don't you think?
Duck, turn, and wink.
Bodies at a distance—
that's what we are,

raises, renovations, Florida,
dinner by the sea.
Look at you.
The waves go swiftly
out of sight—

a long ellipsis
of glaciers swallowing the sun—
come quick, no time for this,
the girls in thongs
are glancing at the clock.

HALFLIFE

The blue square of light
in the window across the street
never goes dark—

the cathodes, the cordage, the atoms
working the hem of dusk—
traveling past the cranes and the docks

and the soiled oyster beds,
the trees loaded with radium,
colors like guns,

red pock-pock red and the sea yellow up,
yellow down—
the blue hour, the waiting.

In the hospitals
I was the light of the TV
I rustled past the guard

I put my hand over your mouth
I shoved your face
into the pillow—

I came through the sodium streets
past the diners, a minister idly turning his glass,
service stations, gas, cars sharp in the light.

How long will the light go on?
Longer than you. Still you ought to live like a city,
rich and fierce at the center.

AT TIGER MOUNTAIN

Bronx Zoo

Exotic, lethargic, dull,
the tigers stretch
along the withered grass.
Look at them;

they don't look back,
except to raise a paw,
their eyes skidding past
like tiger glass. Like tiger glass:

the small blue pool, the
painted asp; little knives
of marsh grass, and strips of meat
sloshing in a feeder's bucket.

Captivity's a hardening.
The tigers stiffen
and prowl like hurricanes
along a coast. They crowd

to eat, coiling their tails;
the big one yawns when full.
Across the river
the sugar sign burns,

the blank night slips sideways
toward us, like a paw
hooked round
an iron bar, velvet and warm.

In the attic I sleep in a swallowing heat.
The green carcasses of beetles line the floorboards;
afternoon creaks through its ecclesiastical hours.

Topriders skim the roof, its tar-hardened cloak,
and light rips west of the mountains, where the neighbor's boy
trips on the enamel hoof of a horse buried in the field.

The rain slipping into the distance, a strange fact.
Our house was built in a valley where the storms
shook it. As if God were thinking of me.

WAR LULLABY

Wet daggers of grass
cast shadows over one another
beneath the porch light—

the boy stretched on the lawn,
fighting sleep,
fingers the tournament ring:

inside the house
his mother shouts, blinds
slap in the breeze,

and upstairs the smallest stir
as they sleep, eyelashes like
tiny whips against their cheeks.

The dogs bark, a door slams,
the boys breathe deep,
then shudder—

I have seen them
sleepwalk
out of the arms of mothers.

SANDY HOOK

The fire burned my cousin here,
first in his bed in the bungalow garage,
then at the lock, scratching in fear.
Quick, quick. The trundle bed
burned. The violin, unpracticed, burned.
The keys of the body, burned. Yellow, red,
the turning leaves. The burning
thing, ablaze, a living shroud: smoke, air, bone,
a licking; then the carbonite no one looks at twice.
The instrument, delinquent with disuse.
Outside, the hooks of the waves twist
and desist, twist and insist,
like coats hung out beneath
the snailing clouds to dry.

ELEGY

Flags breeze over tarmac in the club lot,
      container ships steam up the coast,

smokestacks like cigars
      between the loose lips of the bay.

Your nine iron drawn back for the swing,
      a half chuckle: that's where you left off,

in the surf of bees and grass
      at the twelfth hole, the remnants

of the host beneath your tongue,
      business card in pocket (Vice Pres., *American Shipping*).

Curiosity was your business.
      I ask you to come close.

Footsteps rustle in the witchgrass,
      cotton cuffs switch past, the stalks stir.

How lucky it is I was born
      to tell you the way it all turned out.

II

STILL LIFE AMONGST PARTIAL OUTLINES

I.

Every night, the same:

I wake; here and there
the eye can make out an edge,

the back of a couch;
or the lamp is on

but the light seems sickly.
My mouth sour with wine—

something is in the room with me;
something I can't see.

I look for him, I want to find him
looking for me—

II.

At six, death dropped around me
like a sheet. I was playing tag
with my brother and a friend
whose name I can't recall,
when, out of breath, hungry,

I stopped to rest, put my hands
on the old oak table
(our parents were away) and fit
my fingernail into the slot

where the wood met the decorative lip
bounding it. A cold
ice rooted me
to the linoleum floor,

like a tree in winter.

III.

Far from the dirty bay of the Hudson, far
     from New York's penthouses and gutters,
where the Battenkill rolls among fields of green,
we came to spend the summer; here,
     one day,—the newspaper informs me,
when I am twelve, in 1988—
     "Inside the dense brush and trees
          on an early Vermont spring day in 1981,
               Melissa Walbridge and Meghan O'Rourke,
twelve-year-old friends, were repeatedly raped
     tortured
          and stabbed in a wooded area
behind a town park.
          Remarkably,
Meghan O'Rourke survived the attack
     and was able to describe the attackers . . ."
one of whom, that spring, had been freed—;

—a story that could not be forgotten or owned,
like looking in a mirror and discovering someone else's face.

IV.

In my sleep a garden grew,
a kind I'd never seen before or walked in;

(or so it seemed);

what I had reconciled myself
to losing—the wooden barrette from China,

the Salvation Army sweaters I wore in college,
his lean-faced Anglo-Saxon cussedness—

returned to me, as if the memory had been
transported to the ordinary electric-lit

room in which I sleep, the words
I'd grown used to not uttering, *love*,

so long displaced, a box of letters, vividly present—
like the hum of a power line outside the window

which, now, downed in the storm, wakes you,
buzzing along the street's guardrail into a puddle;

a wire capable of killing a large animal,
like the one that last week silenced a couple

whose car broke down in the flooded road
as they stepped out into the puddle—*zap!*—their bodies

still pliant. Only minutes earlier,
they'd kissed. Her lipstick on his face,

the cracks of her lips wet on his skin.
When I wake my hair is full of static.

Now the garden I walk in at night
is overgrown and uncivilized. All day

the flowers thicken in their sturdy plot,
the honeysuckle climbs, requiring me to stop, and weed.

V.

In another life, he tells me,
we were brothers—twins.
We ran together; we ate
from the same brass bowl, twin lions,
each standing guard for the other
as he fed; we broke our arms
and healed, quickly, skimming rocks
in the morning over the lake.
And now we were here, in Brooklyn, a lariat of blood
between us; our love, so unquiet, unfamilial, was
fraternal: what had connected us
had brought us back together, only
I had chosen—in some past I could not imagine—
to unstitch myself from him, from my own
flesh, and become . . . alien.

And so when I fought with him,
and then returned, a penitent, submissive,
he said, what I wanted
was my own boyhood back—
I wanted to be changed,
like Daphne and the laurel tree. . . .

In his green eyes, I hear his soul
muttering like the ocean
at its farthest edge.

VI.

When you are a child this is all you have:
rules, mountains, pools, boundaries, magic

that doesn't work. What happened to her
did not happen to you. You were a child,

you were safe, you were not harmed. But
there are fields inside us. They grow.

How do you choose which ones to make room for
under the golden sun, and which ones to lock away,

so that men cannot climb into them at twilight,
vaulting over the iron fence

and landing lightly in the grass?
What happens when you invite what you love

into the field and it will not stay?
Is the grass still green, does it continue to grow like grass?

VII.

Even in the winter, his body is warm;
even in the winter, after we have slept like this

for months, I come to with a start, not
        understanding what lies beside me, eyes closed,
warm as a rock warmed by an alien sun;

I have just come from somewhere else—
        where children with uncombed hair
guide me through slanting valleys,

walking arm in arm with me through a corona of snow
        to a barren place: the garden
I still stand half in and half out of,
        and in which, waking,

for a moment, I *see* his face—what was
his face, what would be his face:

                              a cold fox, forgetful
of the place from which we came—

he wakes; he stretches out
a careless arm, and smiles. And tomorrow
he will do the same; and again; and
then not.

VIII.

On a cloudless night, the boys walk
            through the wooded field kicking at tame weeds,
shoes scuffing among the woodchips put down
            along the back path from the fields
to the cluster of houses by Route 4.
            The grass is so tall that cicadas
cling to it as it bends beneath their weight,
            little old men weakly singing,
fate, fate, fate. By whose indifference
            did harm enter the world. . . .

When they come upon the girls

—among dense trees, tall, degraded
grass, goldenrod, daisies—
just begun to bloom—and on a musty
mattress—

when they come upon the girls,
                                the boys
    stop:

One takes out a knife and one takes out a rope.
It is a tired old truth, that death comes to each
the same, to each alone—
a solitary, singular act,
like laying out a tablecloth to eat in solitude—

and all this a few miles from where we pass
on the path to swim
by the culvert
and the river splitting into creeks
like a hand spread over the land.

IX.

My eyes hurt. A translucent sheet
has grown over them.
Twilight intrudes at the edge of the bay, and the room

goes gray—so that one can make out only edges,
the back of a couch, the light at the mantel ledge—
concealing from us the things that have slipped

from our loose grasp—girls combing their hair
with Goody combs, boys running
with baseball gloves outstretched—

and have drifted away, a wave of light
moving out into the last trough of the ocean; a path
that appears to be a way forward,

but is not a way at all, is nothing
but a tendency of light
traveling through the great, cremated distances of autumn.

III

CHECKLIST

There was a lot to be done before I grew.
The flowery bedspread had to go.

Then the voice. *Hello.* I taped myself
getting dressed, mouthing "I understand your concern."

I rose early. I read books
downstairs before anyone was awake.

My parents told me to go outside.
Diving downward through the river.

Glimpses of bridges; peering upward through the blue
as faces climbed away. I wrote it down.

On my hand, a pine tree, sap
you can't wash off. Love.

A line of cars humming down the road in silence. Then silence.
The ditch beside the empty house, the rivulets,

the sun just leaving, the red light
retreating, the sun, the ditch, the house.

I slept and dreamt and slept and dreamt—
I woke, the radiators banged and flaked.
I slept and dreamt, gnawing handkerchiefs
that turned out to be sheets—
my mother had tangled hair
dark and gray as an oak;
she was growing old. In the car
I slept and dreamt, then woke: the shocks were bad.

I woke: I stayed like that, before anything broke,
before she swerved off the shoulder of Route 9,
her hair like cotton in my mouth.
The length of her arm against my arm,
my leg along her leg,
shoulder to shoulder, the car's steel frame made a sound
like very young, very hungry
birds, her flesh drew away
and then pressed on me, as if we slept again together.

In a ditch along which a wire post fence ran,

keeping goldenrod from grass, keeping us

from the soybean field, we woke.

Along the post against which she'd fallen

she ran her fingers restlessly.

Lying next to her, I looked and saw

the letters of my name scratched in the hand of a child—

as if we had been here, years ago,

on an afternoon I do not remember, when

the air smelled of November smoke.

I took my hand like a handkerchief

and wiped her face. I slept, and woke.

The radiator banged, the clock was wet

with midnight sweat.

PRAYER

At this distance—
me, on my knees, the quicklime basin of water,
him, his hands, the water licked from fingers.

But those fingers were not *his* fingers.
They were a form in the room: promise.

THE LIGHTHOUSE KEEPER

My ear, a shell on the pillow;
    the down, the sea from which his mouth arrived.

Strange to live in a wet world, then wake in the desert.
    The cactus on whom milky needles grow.

Let me live offshore, where the water is low.
    Strange, and then so much less so.

I was seventeen. Do you want
    to know what I didn't know?

I do.

LATE MASTERY

So this is happiness: a flaxen, spoiling moon;
blindfolds; teasing, catastrophic fantasies.
Three weights of darkness:
a switch, a flick, a strike. My hands cold
beneath the duck-print eiderdown. That menagerie.
I do not like the sound of bedclothes
sliding to the wax-slick floor.
I do not like your body elsewhere.
And I do not like love, that narrow street,
along which children who play at the gate
disappear for days to return with a smile,
lighting matches in the grass
as if to smell—again—the sulfur.

WINTER PALACE

By my hands I hang in the bedroom
of a man's strange mind.
The walls are lined with fleurs-de-lis
made from the fur of mice.
Smoke climbs in the chimney.

Yet another plague—
in northern pastures long-nosed horses
stamp at the smell of bodies
burning behind the castle.
The rope around my fingers creaks,

moths bang against the window,
a doctor stumbles up the walk—
the corners are full of needles
to help me sleep,
mice lie like kings in their copper traps.

Keep still, he says,
the vein is hard to find
without a little pinch. See?
Supervision is so
much better than freedom.

Morning arrived like a movie screen,
the cold stacked at the edges of my spine.
I woke chewing my own hair;
all I wanted was to be clean.
The stone of the basin
stiffened, the ice stripped the day
chip by chip; you can't see a goddamned thing
under a sky like this. The unsettling dark,
the reeling out. This is how it is.
I can taste the rock, I mean, *taste* it,
between my teeth.
The things the brain does.

SOPHOMORES

I'm a princess with a hole in my heart
—all the plastic deer bend away from me—
and you've got a melancholic bent.
Where did you get the idea to live in a cathedral?
It's America, 1993, and the malls
are cool and clean. Don't you know,
like me, that no one gets out alive?
Still, the guitar rises into the spotlit air,
the ribbons I bought glitter
in their plastic packages. Let's climb
the broken, bat-filled rafters and drape
them from the heights, see how far we can see.

All it was was a knee up against mine
beneath a stone ceiling, gold and alkaline.
A godly mind stuffy as a false drawer.
Or did you really think that you were an angel,
and that in the dark you would be made legible—
the curtained shadows hiding
the wounds, the glibness, the surprise
at finding yourself just a boy whose heart was a size too small,
not a grand catastrophe, after all?

Shadows passed over the statues—
crossed them, hesitated, vanished;
even the dust was white as a bird.

Someone had loved me,
then stopped. I had failed
in a minute but final way;

all the words exchanged
risen past the boundaries
of what had been made

and what wasn't yet outlined, risen
like a parrot toward the sky
only to find a painted ceiling and a stenciled sun.

I lived in a museum, curled
up against a body of stone,
spine to block-gray base

as a stranger's face looked
down upon me,
a bird in someone else's mind.

TROY

We had a drink and got in bed.
That's when the boat in my mouth set sail,
my fingers drifting in the shallows of your buzz cut.
And in the sound of your eye
a skiff coasted—boarding *it*
I found all the bric-a-brac of your attic gloom,
the knives from that other island trip,
the poison suckleroot lifted from God-knows-where.
O all your ill-begotten loot—and yes, somewhere,
the words you never actually spoke,
the woven rope tethering
me to this rotting joint. Touch me,
and the boat and the city burn like whiskey
going down the throat. Or so it goes,
our love-wheedling myth, excessively baroque.

IV

TWO SISTERS

It has been speculated that the children born in such a pregnancy
may have some memories of their vanishing twins. . . .

I.

I let go the hands of the one I slept with,
the wind called, come quick, come quick,
the days are loosening like sticks in the water.

I slept the way the lonely sleep,
uncomfortable, walking through rooms of stone.
I did not arrive for days. In fact, they had to roll up

their white choir-boy sleeves and come after me,
with a lunge of the thumb and a snap of the wrist.
My skin capitulated to the air, it became skin,

my bones fell into their dusty length,
I dropped onto surfaces shinier than I.
Nothing needs me here.

II. The Lost Sister

When you left, a world
came. Rain,

a morning, a weather
that wouldn't end.

The windows closed like stitches.
Fingernails grew; nothing to pick at.

The tent of our mother's body went
wet around me and clung.

When you left
I stayed, I shook!

Like an instrument about
to be played by the long,

liver-yellow
fingers of the sun.

III.

I woke and slept and woke and slept.
And still didn't smell the smoke.
What kind of sister keeps to herself
in the shadows of the grass?

IV. The Lost Sister

I know what you think, in that blank screen
you call a mind. Across which blue images
crawl: horses rooted against green pines.
Or more mundane things—pencils in a chipped vase.
And then, thoughts: spirited explosions,
fading into their own static.

That mind of yours, that screen—
it's so easy to write memories on it.
And so easy to erase them.
They might as well not be yours; how little you know
of your life. The banging snow around
father, on a Tuesday in January of 1982
when your puppy was new, his tail a cigar butt:

See? You don't remember—rich, satisfied, adrift
in a room that might as well be bare,
that is bare until each image
gets tacked by me to the tall walls,
you see? So don't even think you are the half of me.

V.

When I was a girl, I went with my mother to Penn Station. People thronged past holding overstuffed bags. The smell of pretzels yeasty in the air, like new weather, and above in the Garden the circus began. My mother walked past the men loitering and begging, her black hair bobbed, her faux-leopard-spotted coat an orbit of its own.

I could swim underwater. I could make trains rattle with speed—could close my eyes and press the cold center pole in the first car, the living tendril in it, and find what fed. Looking out the front car's soot-smudged window as we came into the station, I saw a bird, a falcon, leap from a man's hand, and sweep forward in the tunnel, unstayed, unrestrained, while I slowed the train in its track.

In the dark we waited just outside the station. The air-conditioning off; the car a dark cloak, sweat sneaking down our chests. I was the finch in the oak tree that never spoke, and had no ambition, not even to sing, its little beak tight, hopping from limb to limb like something that had seen the sun and was still dazed.

VI. The Lost Sister

You came to wake me in the shade of magnolia trees,
your face strange among the resting birds,

and offered me water. I drank, and without sadness
you looked at me lying in the wheat field, and stood me

on my two feet, your hand in my hand,
and walked me to the edge of the woods and said,

Sunlight moves slowly through my house
like sunlight in a painting—

and you may come and look if you would like.
And I could not enter.

VII.

Little one, lost of eye, sister,
today at Sandy Hook I rode
the parabola of tide
into the furthest sandy inlet,
fish quarreling at my feet,
the quick ones getting away
through the rotted gaps of nets,
the two of me sewn together,
for a moment, like a needle and a vein, the sand
a desultory, domesticated home,
the tide coming in, the bone-moon adrift.

VIII. The Lost Sister

She was a master of childhood, very green,
very given to play, very sleepy, very grit of gray.
I, I was a shadow in a tree for no one to see,
I was a piece of ice in a tidal sweep.
When she laughed the sea made order of disorder.
I was a shadow in a tree, a stain
along the thawing bough for no one to see.

In her life, the hours pass casually.
Snow continues to pile on snow,
the dust in the corners of the old farm house
grows like mice in winter.
I, I was the snow that fell too soon,
before the ground had frozen enough to catch me
and make me stick.

WESTPORT CEMETERY

All the rusty tongues
in boxes in the mown earth;
red trumpet-flowers.

HUNT

The light of the mind is red. It is a red street,
it never ends, it must be kept to
like a schedule. When it is fine, it is fine,

and the night's hounds flinch from it.
Foxes run under dark cover of leaves;
the glacier, trapping everything unused, melts.

Everything natural to us must be learned.
The broken laugh, the branching glance,
the wood beneath the green, embarking skin.

The light of the mind is red. It is a red street,
and a cold home stands at its darkening end,
toward which foxes run through clicking leaves.

STILLBORN

The taste of metal, a crimp by the temples,
a buzzing, a filament hemming and hawing—

where you came from children crept out of cots
in the dark, waiting for the sun to slip closer.

Next time I visit, I'll bring some back.
I'm planning to rescue the legends,

the ones who play in the dirt beneath the bridge
and tell me *We have heard of bread.*

The magnolia creaks in the snow.
The buds have already begun, fat pink fingertips.

THERMOPYLAE

Bring me to your childhood room, where
the old captains never flinched, and push me to the floor.
The arrows of the Persians flew so thick
and came so fast they blotted out the sun.
All the better, the captains said; we will fight in the shade.
A far cry from the aunt's needlepoint by the door—
Bless this home and all who visit.
Downstairs the family sleeps like a tapestry;
the soldiers stood till noon, when the clouds parted
and sun drenched the battlefield.
Tiger shadows stripe our twisted legs, and even the books
seem to pull from the sight
of my being stitched to your sleeping limbs,
as if beyond the arrows of leaves
they spot a sun unhorsed from its chariot,
head to your breakable head, the shapes
across the pass at first indistinct,
then stiffened into bodies, limbs, thumbs.
One hand running over the bruised ridges of the wound,
the other tugging at the stiff black thread.

SIGNAL FIRES
for M.

The horse staggers out of my sleep.
I follow him with my eye
down the blacktop past the football
field, his hooves clipping his knees,
I follow until I've climbed on his slippery back.
We ride like this for miles, nights.
Galloping past the rum hibiscus
and into the green moraines,
where we eat hard blue grass and
I begin to pray. O home!

Our father never rode horses,
not even in his sleep, one hand curled on the arm chair,
the other propping up his head,
cushioning his ears from the sound of windblown wheat.
But he, he was a horse from Troy,
a tinder, a tender, a ruse, a quack, a doctor.
A doctor! A man with a daughter upstairs
like a banked fire, a man with five daughters,
all like quiet fires, crackling and breathing,
until the four black horses
arrive at our buttoned windows,
with their soft brown eyes, and the cold noses
with which they sniff.

The dog did no harm.
The bee did no harm.
The grass, the grave grass, no harm.
The wind did no harm.

The mud did no harm.
The fly, the sticky fly, no harm.
The snakes did not hurt us.
The trees did not either.

The sky, no harm, the moon,
no harm. The wild cats of San Juan,
sleeping in the wet harbor,
did no harm!

The river did no harm.
The land kept going green.
It is bright here, where we sleep
by the lake. Let us pause

to praise the warm, cool
light as it bends
around the unharmed earth,
our faces buried in the woollen dark—

How could you think
it would hurt us? What made you worry?
That whisper the earth makes, turning in space?
I hear it too. It only does what it must.

So hush, hush, hush.

PALIMPSEST

So the days go by, and the singing at night continues.
The summer passes like horses.
Wisdom arrives on a piece of paper, blown
through wide glass windows:
"This page intentionally left blank."
I talk to my friends more than I used to.
I sleep less. This is the point of life:
you really care. The tendons slacken,
the fat honeycombs beneath the skin,
a fox paces in the town courtyard,
until, passing a mirror, on the phone,
laughing, you see yourself again
as you are, as you are not.
The snow creaks underfoot.
Touch me, I am still here,
like the humming bee, like the mayrope
wrapped around the tree.
The song was never mine to sing.
It lives beneath the skin.
It speaks in every bone.

SPECTACULAR

Once something must have happened here,
before you were always quoting yourself to sleep,
needing to remember. Gunpowder
boomed in the birch forests,
redcoats flashed like flowers.
The city was narcotic with gold,
derricks stiffened beside wounded ships.
Women wept for the diving bells of dead.
Flames rose along the river, longing—

All that is green must turn to red.
Listen: the dynamite cracks
in the concrete forest.
That echo is the sound of borrowed grace. Believe it,
ask memory to be your burning stake.

INVENTING A HORSE

Inventing a horse is not easy.
One must not only think of the horse.
One must dig fence posts around him.
One must include a place where horses like to live;

or do when they live with humans like you.
Slowly, you must walk him in the cold;
feed him bran mash, apples;
accustom him to the harness;

holding in mind even when you are tired
harnesses and tack cloths and saddle oil
to keep the saddle clean as a face in the sun;
one must imagine teaching him to run

among the knuckles of tree roots,
not to be skittish at first sight of timber wolves,
and not to grow thin in the city,
where at some point you will have to live;

and one must imagine the absence of money.
Most of all, though: the living weight,
the sound of his feet on the needles,
and, since he is heavy, and real,

and sometimes tired after a run
down the river with a light whip at his side,
one must imagine love
in the mind that does not know love,

an animal mind, a love that does not depend
on your image of it,
your understanding of it;
indifferent to all that it lacks:

a muzzle and two black eyes
looking the day away, a field empty
of everything but witchgrass, fluent trees,
and some piles of hay.

KNIVES OF LIGHT

I.

In his studio, on a canvas stretched and primed,
Bonnard kept bits of silver paper
to catch light: so he could work
in the poorest-lit hotel or friend's home.
Mes brillants, he called the bits.

He rose, moved to the window, looked out
into the yellow crescent of lamplight, surprised
by what he'd made. Outside, the leaves turned from leaves.

II.

In the variable light of my room
I stand and in the wind the curtains stir.
And in the room I see.
The mind is a stony landscape, which replaces
need with rock, fact with fact,
but does not flourish beyond itself:
is how it always was, bare, wide, cracked,
capable of knowing small, neat things.

Shortly before his death, Bonnard wrote,
"I am only beginning to understand.
I should start all over again."
Bits of silver turn in the breeze,
knives of light and appetite.
They want to be used.

NOTES

"Meditations on a Moth": *High and Low* is a film by Akira Kurosawa.

"My Life as a Teenager": The poem contains a quotation from Malcolm Cowley's *Exile's Return*.

"A Further Sea": The title is borrowed from Emily Dickinson.

"Still Life Amongst Partial Outlines": Section III of the poem draws its quoted language from news accounts in Vermont newspapers.

"Two Sisters": The epigraph is taken from a Wikipedia entry on Vanishing Twin Syndrome.

"Hunt": The line "Everything natural to us must be learned" is translated loosely from Hölderlin.

"Thermopylae": The title refers to the site of a battle between the Spartans and the Persians in 480 B.C., in which the outnumbered Spartans fought to their death in a mountain pass to buy time for the evacuation of Athens.

"Knives of Light": The painter Pierre Bonnard did keep bits of paper he called "*brillants*" with him when he traveled. The quotation is taken from his papers.